LEONARD J. ARRINGTON
MORMON HISTORY LECTURE SERIES
No. 24

REDEEMING A PEOPLE

by Darius Gray

Sponsored by

Special Collections & Archives
Merrill-Cazier Library
Utah State University
Logan, Utah

Published by Merrill-Cazier Library
Distributed by Utah State University Press
Logan, UT 84322

FOREWORD

F. Ross Peterson

The establishment of a lecture series honoring a library's special collections and a donor to that collection is unique. Utah State University's Merrill-Cazier Library houses the personal and historical collection of Leonard J. Arrington, a renowned scholar of the American West. As part of Arrington's gift to the university, he requested that the university's historical collection become the focus for an annual lecture on an aspect of Mormon history. Utah State agreed to the request and in 1995 inaugurated the annual Leonard J. Arrington Mormon History Lecture.

Utah State University's Special Collections and Archives is ideally suited as the host for the lecture series. The state's land grant university began collecting records very early, and in the 1960s became a major depository for Utah and Mormon records. Leonard and his wife Grace joined the USU faculty and family in 1946, and the Arringtons and their colleagues worked to collect original diaries, journals, letters, and photographs.

Although trained as an economist at the University of North Carolina, Arrington became a Mormon historian of international repute. Working with numerous colleagues, the Twin Falls, Idaho, native produced the classic *Great Basin Kingdom: An Economic History of the Latter-day Saints* in 1958. Utilizing available collections at USU, Arrington embarked on a prolific publishing and editing career. He and his close ally, Dr. S. George Ellsworth, helped organize the Western History Association, and they created the *Western Historical Quarterly* as the scholarly voice of the WHA.

While serving with Ellsworth as editor of the new journal, Arrington also helped both the Mormon History Association and the independent journal *Dialogue*.

One of Arrington's great talents was to encourage and inspire other scholars or writers. While he worked on biographies or institutional histories, he employed many young scholars as researchers. He fostered many careers as well as arranged for the publication of numerous books and articles.

In 1972, Arrington accepted appointments as the official historian of the Church of Jesus Christ of Latter-day Saints and the Lemuel Redd Chair of Western History at Brigham Young University. More and more Arrington focused on Mormon, rather than economic, historical topics. His own career flourished with the publication of *The Mormon Experience*, co-authored with Davis Bitton, and *American Moses: A Biography of Brigham Young*. He and his staff produced many research papers and position papers for the LDS Church as well. Nevertheless, tension developed over the historical process, and Arrington chose to move full time to BYU with his entire staff. The Joseph Fielding Smith Institute of History was established, and Leonard continued to mentor new scholars as well as publish biographies. He also produced a very significant two-volume study, *The History of Idaho*.

After Grace Arrington passed away, Leonard married Harriet Horne of Salt Lake City. They made the decision to deposit the vast Arrington collection of research documents, letters, files, books, and journals at Utah State University. The Leonard J. Arrington Historical Archives is part of the university's Special Collections. The Arrington Lecture Committee works with Special Collections to sponsor the annual lecture.

REDEEMING A PEOPLE

The formal title of this lecture is *Redeeming a People: The Critical Role of Historical Examination in Moving Cultural and Moral Trajectories.* That's a pretty lofty title, but with your indulgence, we'll take a look at the importance of being informed about our history and how that history has affected us and those with whom we associate.

We are here to discuss this subject as a result of an event that took place in June 1978, which was the announcement by The Church of Jesus Christ of Latter-day Saints that revelation had been received by Spencer W. Kimball, the prophet and president of the Church at that time.

The following is taken from the Church's website:

> In early June 1978, the Lord revealed to President Spencer W. Kimball that the priesthood should be given to all worthy male members of the Church. This made the priesthood available to all worthy men and temple blessings available to all worthy members, regardless of race or color. On September 30, 1978, this declaration was presented to the general conference of the Church and unanimously accepted.[1]

On June 1, 2018, we celebrated the 40th anniversary of that event, an event that arguably has given us greater cause for celebration than many may know.

As with much of history, the actual effects of events are most remembered, and felt, by those who lived through them. Many in the reading audience may not have been born in 1978, and many others may have been too young to appreciate the significance of what occurred. The view from 40,000 feet, or from forty years afterward, can be less detailed than the view from ground level.

Let's consider the critical nature of that historic change in policy by noting what life was like on the ground and in the weeds, so to speak, during the years that preceded President Kimball's revelation.

My purpose is not to take a lengthy look at the past for the sake of laying blame or of speaking ill of persons in the past. Rather, we must examine history to better understand the magnificence of the changes ushered in by that revelation. I again direct your attention to the title of this lecture:

> *Redeeming a People: The Critical Role of Historical Examination in Moving Cultural and Moral Trajectories*

And move we have!

We live in a secular world, and as would be expected, worldly attitudes frequently have affected the many religious communities in that world. Therefore, a sincere examination of religious history is benefited by factoring in the dynamics generated from the secular.

As the constitution of this nation was being formulated during the Constitutional Convention of 1787 in Philadelphia, an argument arose about proportional representation based on population. The Southern slave states wanted slaves included in the count; the Northern free states did not. Compromise thus created the 3/5 clause, by which each slave was to be considered 3/5th of a human being. The general devaluing of the Negro as human was codified.

Of the fifty-five delegates attending the convention, nearly half (twenty-five) owned slaves.

We move quickly now to the year 1857. That year a ruling was handed down by the Supreme Court of the United States in the case of a slave named Dred Scott versus his owner, John Sanford. Mr. Scott had been a slave in Missouri but had journeyed with his then-owner, a Mr. Emerson, to the free state of Illinois and then to Wisconsin Territory. There an earlier act of Congress, the Missouri Compromise, had barred slavery. Upon being returned to Missouri, Mr. Scott filed suit for his freedom from the man who now owned him, Mr. Sanford.

The Supreme Court did not rule in Dred Scott's favor. The broadness of the decision was disastrous for those seeking freedom from slavery for themselves or others:

1. Neither Dred Scott nor any other slave could become free by virtue of residence in a free state or territory;
2. Negroes, slave or free, were not citizens and therefore did not have the right to sue in federal court; and
3. Under the Constitution, Congress did not have the power to exclude slavery from the western territories and therefore the Missouri Compromise was unconstitutional. Slaves were property, and the government could not violate a slave owner's right to property by prohibiting slavery in the territories.

Not only was that landmark decision in 1857 a significant setback for freedom, what was written in it by the Court's Chief Justice, Roger B. Taney, was possibly even more damaging. He wrote:

> They (the Negro) had for more than a century before been regarded as beings of an inferior race, and altogether unfit to associate with the white races, either in social or political relations; and so far inferior that they had no rights which the white man was bound to respect, and that the Negro might justly and lawfully be reduced to slavery for his benefit.[2]

Those words and the attitudes that gave rise to them cankered the nation's soul and just as surely wrested humanity from the majority as surely as humanness had been stripped from the minority.

Our quick journey down the lane of American history may have left you wondering what any of that has to do with President Kimball's revelation and the celebration of the 40th anniversary of its reception. To make that connection clearer, let us look further into the influence a secular society can have on a religious community.

In 1895 Elder B. H. Roberts, of the Church's First Council of the Seventy, wrote in New Witnesses for God:

> It was obvious to the Europeans when they first beheld the natives of America, that these were unlike the intellectual white-skinned race of Europe, the barbarous blacks of Africa, or any nation or people which they had hitherto encountered.[3]

Elder Bruce R. McConkie, then an assistant to the Church's Quorum of the Twelve Apostles, wrote in 1958:

> In a broad general sense, caste systems have their root and origin in the gospel itself, and when they operate according to the divine decree, the resultant restrictions and segregation are right and proper and have the approval of the Lord. All this is not to say that any race, creed, or caste should be denied any inalienable rights. But it is to say that Deity in his infinite

wisdom, to carry out his inscrutable purposes, has a caste system of his own, a system of segregation of races and peoples. . . . It is only by a knowledge of pre-existence that it can be known why some persons are born in one race or caste and some in another.[4]

Perhaps the only statements more stunning than that of Chief Justice Taney were two made by the third Church president, John Taylor. The first was made August 28, 1881:

> And after the flood we are told that the curse that had been pronounced upon Cain was continued through Ham's wife, as he had married a wife of that seed. And why did it pass through the flood? Because it was necessary that the devil should have a representation upon the earth as well as God.[5]

The second statement was made October 29, 1882:

> Why is it that good men should be tried? Why is it, in fact, that we should have a devil? Why did not the Lord kill him long ago? Because he could not do without him. He needed the devil and a great many of those who do his bidding just to keep men straight, that we may learn to place our dependence upon God, and trust in Him, and to observe his laws and keep his commandments. When he destroyed the inhabitants of the antediluvian world, he suffered a descendant of Cain to come through the flood in order that he might be properly represented upon the earth.[6]

These were the same citations, but again, my purpose is not to shock but to present context for why the revelation of 1978 was so profound.

The next part of our Church history might provide unexpected information, but it is an accurate representation of that history. We recall two black elders of the 1800s who served as missionaries and one of whom served as the first president of the Boston, Massachusetts, branch of the Church: Joseph T. Ball Jr. and Elijah Abel. We note also Jane Harris Dykes, a black sister who in 1895 was sealed in the Salt Lake Temple to her white husband.

First, let us consider Joseph T. Ball Jr., who was born February 21, 1804, in Cambridge, Middlesex County, Massachusetts. His mother, Mary Montgomery Drew of Cambridge, Massachusetts, was white. His father, Joseph T. Ball Sr., was born in Jamaica and moved to Massachusetts in 1790, where six years later he became the founder of a society to help African-American widows in need.

Joseph T. Ball Jr. was baptized into The Church of Jesus Christ of Latter-day Saints in the summer of 1832 by either Brigham Young or his brother Joseph Young in Boston. Soon after his baptism, in September 1833, Joseph Ball moved to Kirtland, Ohio, where he became acquainted with the Prophet Joseph Smith. He may have been ordained an elder as early as 1833 or as late as 1837. Wilford Woodruff, an early Church leader, remembered that Ball was an elder in 1837 when they served a mission together in New England and New Jersey.

In 1843 Ball was ordained a high priest by William Smith, brother of Joseph Smith. Ball served as president of the Boston branch of the Church from October 1844 to March 1845. The Boston congregation was the largest group of members of the Church outside Church headquarters in Nauvoo, Illinois. Not only was he the first African-American to be ordained a high priest in the Church, but he was also the first black man to preside over a congregation within that church.

In the spring of 1845, after Ball's service as branch president was concluded, apostle Parley P. Pratt sent him to Nauvoo to work on the temple there and promised him that there he would receive his temple endowment. While in Nauvoo, Ball received his patriarchal blessing from William Smith and participated in the ordinance of baptisms for the dead in behalf of his ancestors.

In August 1845 both Ball and William Smith left the Church for reasons that are unclear. Because Ball left the Church before the Nauvoo Temple was completed, he did not receive his temple endowment. After leaving Nauvoo, Ball appears to have affiliated with a Mormon schismatic group in Wisconsin led by James Strang and appears in the records of that group in 1848. Joseph T. Ball Jr. died of tuberculosis on September 20, 1861, in Boston, Massachusetts. He was buried in Cambridge, Massachusetts, where the Ball family plot lies.[7]

Next we consider Elijah Abel, possibly the best known of the early black Latter-day Saint priesthood holders. His missionary certificate was signed by Joseph Smith. The text reads:

> To Whom It May Concern:
>
> This certifies that Elijah Abel has been received into the church of the Latter Day Saints, organized on the sixth of April, in the year of our Lord one thousand, eight hundred & thirty, and has been ordained an Elder according to the rules and regulations of said church, & is duly authorized to preach the gospel agreeable to the authority of that office. From the satisfactory evidence which we have of his good moral character, & his zeal for the cause of righteousness, & diligent desire to persuade men to forsake evil

& embrace truth, we confidently recommend him to all candid & upright people as a worthy member of society. We therefore, in the name, & by the authority of this church grant unto this, our worthy brother in the Lord this letter of commendation as a proof of our fellowship & Esteem: Praying for his success and prosperity in our Redeemer's Cause given by the direction of a conference of the Elders of said Church assembled in Kirtland, Geauga County, Ohio, the third day of March, in the year of our Lord one thousand, eight hundred & thirty-six.

> [signed] Joseph Smith, Jr., Chairman.
> F. G. Williams, Clerk.
> Kirtland, Ohio, March 31, 1836.

Sister Eunice Kinney of Flintville, Wisconsin, spoke most favorably of Elder Abel in a letter written September 1891 to a Brother Watson, Bay Springs, Michigan:

> My Testimony of the Latter-day Work
>
> I have many times, in the years that is past and gone, felt impressed to give my testimony in regard to the great and glorious work of the last days. I have neglected this duty until I feel that my journey in this life will soon close. I will soon be seventy-nine years old, I am very feeble, not able to write as I would wish. Therefore, I shall be very brief and only note the most important items of my experiences.
>
> In the spring of 1838 I heard the first Gospel sermon by a latter-day Saint. His name was Elijah Abel; he was ordained by Joseph, the martyred prophet. I was then living in the town of Madrid, Lawrence County, New York. We had never heard of the latter-day Saints until Elder Abel came into the place. I, with my husband, went and heard him preach. Abel was a man without education; it was difficult for him to read his text but when he commenced to preach, the Spirit rested upon him and he preached a most powerful sermon. It was such a Gospel sermon as I had never heard before, and I felt in my heart that he was one of God's chosen ministers. . .
>
> While he was preaching, a great and marvelous change came over me. All the doubts and fears and unbelief and the powerful darkness that had so distressed me fled before the light of God's truth like the dew before the Sun. The Holy Spirit came upon me and I was in a glorious vision. It was then and there made known to me by the power of God that Joseph Smith was a true Prophet of God, and The Book of Mormon was a sacred record of divine origin, and Elijah Abel was a servant of the most high God. I've never had a doubt of these things from that day to this, and when I think of that glorious event it fills my heart with joy and gratitude to my Heavenly Father for such an expression of his goodness.

Brother Abel now had to leave us and go back to Canada to meet his appointments there, but said that he would come and preach to us again in two weeks. But before the two weeks were up, persecution was raging in a fearful manner. Handbills were pasted up in every direction stating the Mormon Elder had murdered a woman and five children and a great reward was offered for him.

We were members of the Methodist Church at the time we united with the Latter-day Saints, and our Methodist brethren were our greatest persecutors. They said to us, 'now, what do you think of your Mormon Elder after committing such a crime?' Said that he would never show himself there again.

I says, 'he will come and fill his appointment and God will protect him.' They said that just as sure as he did come he would not have the privilege of preaching, for they would nab him too quick, but they knew that he would never be seen there again. When the time was nearly up, Elder Abel came and the house was well filled. After Abel was seated a few moments, he rose and says to the congregation, 'my friends, I'm advertised for murdering a woman and five children and a great reward is offered for my person. Now here I am; if anyone has anything to do with me, now is your time. But after I commence my services, don't you dare to lay your hands on me.' He waited in silence a few moments, and no one moved the tongue or raised the hand.

He then opened the meeting with singing and prayer, and he preached a most powerful sermon. He went home with us to stay for the night. The next day he left unmolested.[8]

Our last, but certainly not least, significant person from the past is Jane Harris Dykes. Information about Sister Dykes was given to me by my dear friend Marie Taylor, a diligent researcher of Mormon genealogy:

Jane Harris was Jane Manning James's contemporary. By superimposing their lives on each other, you get a much greater understanding of Jane James's and other black members' frustration over this issue. It also puts a much clearer perspective on why Jane James kept petitioning the brethren for permission to receive her temple ordinances.

Jane Harris Dykes was born in 1821 on the Island of St. Helena. She joined the Church in Africa, then came to Zion. Unlike other black Church members, she was endowed and sealed to her husband on October 16, 1895, in the Salt Lake Temple. Over the next number of years she performed proxy ordinances for hundreds of her ancestors.

Why? Because her patriarchal blessing said she was of the tribe of Ephraim. For a while, Church leaders felt that any person of the tribe of Ephraim was not included in the restriction from the priesthood or temple ordinances.

Information like this leaves some room for the idea that the brethren really didn't understand the reason for the restriction (despite what they may have said at the time), because they vacillated from time to time on how they should administer the policy. In fact, these rulings are actually contrary to the reasons they said were the cause of the restriction or who the restriction was for.[9]

Our look at the confluence of American secular history and the history of the Church of Jesus Christ regarding blacks of African descent comes to a close. I hope you've noted the similarities in secular and religious attitudes about blacks—Negroes, as we were called back then. Once again I return us to the formal title of this lecture, *Redeeming a People: The Critical Role of Historical Examination in Moving Cultural and Moral Trajectories.*

Our knowledge of crucial events, ordinations, and sealings is far, far greater today than previously. Not only were important facts forgotten or misplaced but human shortcomings edged their way in by diluting and confusing actual truth with what was assumed to have been.

The wisdom of a friend of mine, Brother Ben Diamond, shone through in a recent conversation we had about this lecture when he said to me:

> The bold transparency of Leonard Arrington's research prepared us for the age of the internet and the high volume of information available for and against the Church. Had he not forged the way ahead, we might not be as prepared as we now are.

Significant events have occurred on the national secular front as well as in the worldwide religious arena. Events that I never expected to see, or even dreamt of seeing, have been front and center. I refer you to the year 2018. It was a monumental year for The Church of Jesus Christ of Latter-day Saints. We witnessed history unfold before us in ways I doubt most of us would have expected.

Sadly, in January 2018 the not unexpected occurred with the passing of Church President Thomas S. Monson. He had served as a general authority since October 1963 and as a counselor to Presidents Ezra Taft Benson, Howard W. Hunter, and Gordon B. Hinckley before being called to the helm himself in February 2008.

In the tradition of our faith, we were comforted in the sorrow of our loss by the calling and sustaining of a new president and prophet. This new prophet, President Russell M. Nelson, hit the ground running—and he must have been wearing cleated track shoes as events have seldom moved forward so quickly in the Mormon church.

The month of May 2018 ushered in a confluence of two historic organizations when the national leadership of the nation's oldest civil rights organization, the NAACP, met with President Nelson and other senior leaders of the Church of Jesus Christ! Wow! I bet you didn't see that one coming.

That was only the beginning. More was yet to come in the form of a celebration marking the 40th anniversary of the world-changing revelation that affected not only that particular day but the past as well as the future.

On the first day of June 2018, exactly forty years after President Spencer W. Kimball's receipt of the revelation on priesthood, the Conference Center in Salt Lake City, Utah, was awash in nothing less than a spiritual high, wrapped in jubilation, and garnished by messages of inclusion.

Present were thousands of celebrants (not all of them Latter-day Saints), a mixture from God's garden of humanity—black and white, male and female, young and old—and they were joined by the entire First Presidency and the complete Quorum of the Twelve Apostles.

Also on the stand with those Church leaders were the ten women and men, persons of color, who had served as the planning committee for the event. That night History, with a capital H, was made.

Setting aside the pain of the past and now having a grander appreciation for the changes ushered in on June 1, 1978, and their commemoration in June 2018, we remember the mileposts along the road to revelation and to the "Be One" celebration.

My membership in The Church of Jesus Christ of Latter-day Saints is now in its 54th year. During that period of time there have been monumental changes in our nation, as well as those undreamt-of changes in the Church. Not surprisingly, the secular and the religious have often been reflections of each other. That, together with their shared history, helps us now to better understand and better appreciate the monumental significance of the 40th anniversary of that world-changing revelation.

The ornamental plates behind exterior doorknobs on the Salt Lake Temple make the connection between what we have just experienced and what the Saints of the 1800s experienced. "This forty-year timespan is paralleled by the forty years that ancient Israel wandered in the wilderness before entering their land of inheritance (see Numbers 14:26–34). When Wilford Woodruff led the saints into the Salt Lake Temple to dedicate it to the Most High God, some who were present compared it to Joshua leading the children of Israel into the promised land."[10]

Forty years to journey in the wilderness of the Sinai Peninsula, forty years of labor to complete the house of the Lord, and forty years to pause and recall all that has come before—the hopes, the joys, the pains, and the sorrows. All so that the future would be brighter than the past.

ENDNOTES

1. See churchofjesuschrist.org.
2. The text of Chief Justice Taney's opinion is available at https://www.loc.gov/item/17001543/. See also The Dred Scott Decision: Opinion of Chief Justice Taney, with an Introduction by Dr. J. H. Van Evrie, at http://www.loc.gov/resource/llst.022.
3. B. H. Roberts, New Witnesses for God, 3 vols. (1895), 3:83.
4. Bruce R. McConkie, Mormon Doctrine, 2nd ed. (1966), 114, "Caste System."
5. John Taylor, in Journal of Discourses, vols. (1854–86), 22:304.
6. John Taylor, in Journal of Discourses, 26 vols. (1854–86), 23:336.
7. Connell O'Donovan, "Plural Marriage and African American Mormons: Race, Schism, and the Beginnings of Priesthood and Temple Denial in 1847," unpublished paper; private possession.
8. Eunice Kinney to Brother Watson, September 1891, is available at https://researchworks.oclc .org/archivegrid/collection/data/367943822.
9. Marie Taylor to Darius A. Gray, emails November 25 and 27, 2000; private possession.
10. Matthew B. Brown and Paul Thomas Smith, Symbols in Stone: Symbolism on the Early Temples of the Restoration (1997), 148.